GOOD DOG!

THE EASY WAY TO TRAIN YOUR DOG

GOOD DOG!

THE EASY WAY TO TRAIN YOUR DOG

SARAH WHITEHEAD

COLLINS & BROWN

First published in the United Kingdom in 2011 by
Collins & Brown
10 Southcombe Street
London W14 0RA

An imprint of Anova Books Company Ltd

Distributed in the United States and Canada by
Sterling Publishing Co, 387 Park Avenue South, New York, NY 10016-8810, USA

All information is correct at time of going to press.

ISBN 978-1-84340-628-0

A CIP catalogue for this book is available from the British Library.

10 9 8 7 6 5 4 3 2 1

Produced by SP Creative Design
All photography by Tim Rose with the exception of the following:
Rolando Ugolini: pages 2, 6, 14, 16, 19, 22, 28, 34, 90, 99 (top), 110, 114, 115 and 116.

Acknowledgements
The publishers would like to thank the following: dog handlers Suzanne Bullworthy, Clare Hamilton, Karen Moore and Sarah Whitehead with her two dogs Tao and Jackson; and the people who let us photograph their dogs: Sue Mothersdale and Hobbs, Mary Coulthurst and Septimus, Jayne Coker and Miya, Michelle Gedling and Paddy, Toni Rae and Marley, Jill Matthews and Willow, Clare McCabe and Trip and Skye, Sharlene Cavanagh and Tula, Fernando Brown and Rodney, Digger and Scruffy, Clare Williams and Charlie, Jacqui MacCarthy and Daisy, Gill Naji and Manson, Karen Tennant and Megan, Ruth Gallagher and Ellie, Anna Walter and Archie, Chiraj Patel and Cody, Laura Russell and Dudley, Sue Mark and Boozy and Tipsey, Karen Napthine and Conor and Enya, June Williams and Pepper, Stella Bagshaw and Kite, and Julie Daniels and Poppy.

Reproduction by Rival Colour Ltd, UK
Printed and bound by 1010 Printing International Ltd, China

This book can be ordered direct from the publisher at www.anovabooks.com

Sarah Whitehead runs the Clever Dog Company, training puppies and dogs based on the most modern methods of teaching. She is a member of the APBC (Association of Pet Behaviour Counsellors) and MD of Alpha Education – an organisation providing accredited education in the field of behaviour and training. She has written several bestselling books on dog training.

CONTENTS

CHAPTER 1
YOUR TRAINING PHILOSOPHY

Dog training should be fun, simple, fast and effective.
Your dog should look forward to training sessions as
if they were games – and so should you. Whatever your
aims for your training – as an obedience competitor,
agility aficionado or simply the owner of a well-behaved
pet – your methods should be enjoyable to keep you and
your dog motivated. Planning is key, so think about what
you want to achieve and structure the sessions accordingly.
Training is all about clever strategy – not bullish tactics.

RELATIONSHIP MATTERS

Does your dog pull on the lead, ignore your commands, sleep on the sofa and eat before you? You may have read that this is because your dog is being 'dominant' and needs to know who's boss but is this really the case? Are dogs challenging their owners for leadership when they show such behaviours, or is something else at work?

Leader or team player?

The 'dominance myth' is a highly attractive one. Based on the fact that dogs are descended from wolves, it states that they see human families as 'packs' with linear hierarchies. We are led to believe that dogs will try to climb up the ladder of rank and challenge us for status. However, domestic dogs are not wolves, any more than we are the same as our ape ancestors. Instead, our pets show far more juvenile characteristics, physiologically and behaviourally, than their wild cousins. This means they are not constantly in competition with

As social beings, dogs are team players. They are happiest when they are working with you and using their natural instincts to your mutual benefit.

us but behave as part of a family group – as members of a close-knit team.

Team-building involves trust and a close working relationship. It relies on the understanding that each member of the team has their own different skills, and whereas one member may be regarded as the decision-maker, he or she relies on the willing efforts of the whole group – something that can never be achieved through force or conflict. Building a positive relationship with your dog enhances every aspect of your training together. A dog that trusts his owner will be confident, calm and co-operative. That's teamwork!

Rewards, rewards...
Keep the motivation and the rewards coming and your dog will want to work hard for you. When he has learned a task, you can cut back on the rewards, but, just like us, dogs need to know that there's a 'salary' waiting, which is worth working for.

Just like us, our dogs need a 'salary' as their motivation to work – a loving bond with their owner is essential, too.

HoUSE RULES

Moving away from imposing a set of 'dominance rules' does not mean being out of control. Indeed, clear signals are essential for dogs, so they can understand which behaviours get rewarded. They respond best to a secure relationship with their owner, sensible 'house rules' and positive, reward-based training. This recipe for success is not based on a power struggle but on consistency and boundaries. What these are will depend on your dog and your specific needs.

Handling

It is essential that dogs willingly allow humans to handle them. All dogs need to cope with being touched by people, simply because veterinary examination, grooming and being moved are all part of everyday life for a pet dog. Handling should always start as early as possible in a puppy's life, and it should be associated with things that he finds pleasurable.

Learning impulse control

Learning to wait patiently is such an intrinsic part of human development that we rarely consider how important it is for dogs, too. Children have to learn to wait for food, attention, and things they want – and it's the same for dogs. Teaching your dog to wait politely for his dinner, to take treats without snatching and be restrained even when he's excited are essential aspects of basic manners training.

Like children, dogs need to learn how to control themselves. This will help them to fit in with our social systems.

Consistency

Mutual respect needs to be earned. One of the easiest ways to establish this is via consistency. Try to decide on your own house rules and ensure that the whole family sticks to them. For instance, if you don't want your dog to lie on the sofa, don't allow him to discover its comforts. Bear in mind that cute puppies grow up into big, strong dogs, so do not let them practise any behaviour when they are young that you don't want them to engage in as adults.

Fitting it into your day

Time – there's never enough of it. Setting aside even ten minutes a day for training your dog can be difficult. The solution lies in breaking down your training sessions into two- or three-minute blocks. Putting the kettle on to make a cup of coffee? That's 90 seconds. Watching TV? Train your dog in the advertisement breaks. Got to go upstairs to collect something? Ask your dog to do a 'sit stay' at the bottom while he waits for you to come back down again. Integrating training into your daily routine is an effective way to achieve great results.

Simple practical management is often the key to consistency and boundaries, such as using a baby gate.

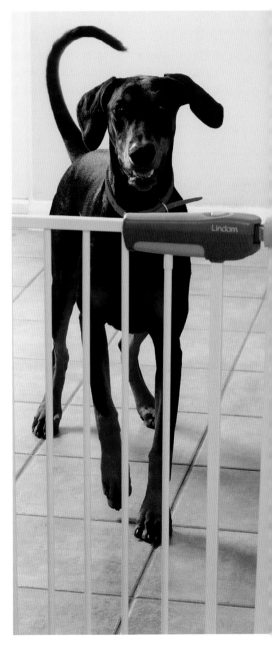

BONDING TIME

Often overlooked as a part of training, attachment is an all-important part of building a good working relationship with your dog. Building a bond with a dog – even a puppy – does not happen overnight. Just like any new friendship, you need to learn about each other's ways, likes and dislikes, and to accept any inherent traits. Bonding doesn't rely just on giving your dog his dinner. Although using food rewards in training is fast and effective, it should be looked on as a tool rather than as a means to an end in gaining your dog's trust and affection.

Affection

How does your dog like to be touched? Away from training, touch can be a wonderful way of simply bonding with your dog. Many dogs prefer to be stroked on the chest and tummy, rather than their heads or backs – and many actively dislike being touched on their feet or tails. Make it your mission to find out where your dog enjoys being petted the most and spend time each day giving mini-massages – it will de-stress you, too.

Play

Those that play together, stay together. Playing games with your dog is an integral and healthy way to bond. Team mates aren't concerned with winning – it's the quality and balance of the game that counts. Tug games, (see page 116), fetch (see page 94), and searching (see page 98) are all part of essential playtime that your dog will love.

Confidence

Dogs who have lots of contact with the outside world tend to be better balanced and more able to deal with new events and experiences than those who have a limited existence. Taking your dog out and about allows him to meet and mix with many other people, dogs and even other animals. Such a wide exposure with you by his side helps to build his confidence, and with that comes a calm acceptance of all that life has to offer.

Opposite: This owner and her dog out on a country walk are in perfect harmony! Creating such a mutually rewarding relationship is worth the time and effort.

CHAPTER 2

HOW DOGS LEARN

Why do dogs do what they do? Because they get rewarded for it. Dogs only repeat certain behaviours if they receive a reward, but that's where the difference in our communication methods can cause problems. We tend to think that giving a dog a treat, or patting him on the head, is a reward. Of course, most dogs like these things – especially food, which is very useful in training – but rewards come in three forms: human attention, internal pleasure (food treats), and external (often 'accidental') rewards from their environment, such as when they knock over a rubbish bin in the kitchen and then proceed to eat the contents.

MOTIVATION AND REWARDS

What gets rewarded gets repeated. The key to successful training is knowing how to motivate your dog and understanding his individual likes and dislikes. For instance, does your dog prefer a piece of cheese or chicken, or would he value an exciting game with a toy?

Which reward works best

All dogs prefer different things and, while it is safe to make some breed assumptions, you should always check with the individual dog. For example, Labradors usually adore food and would most likely prefer a delicious piece of frankfurter to anything else. However, a terrier may prefer an energetic tug game with a rag toy. Collies may have a preference for chase games or fetching items, and even tiny dogs, who may look as if they will work for love alone, will need motivation, too.

As well as tasty titbits, you can reward your dog with an exciting game with a toy.

Motivational rewards

Just like humans, dogs weigh up rewards and judge their behaviour against them. You can try using small pieces of the dry dog food that make up part of your dog's daily ration for run-of-the-mill behaviours, and save the top-level goodies for more difficult exercises. Tiny, pea-sized pieces of hot dog sausage, cubes of cheese or small chunks of chicken are popular with most dogs.

What gets rewarded will get repeated! Be strategic and make sure that your dog is always rewarded for good behaviour, and use management to avoid bad behaviour and prevent it becoming a habit.

Jackpot!

There are some occasions when your dog deserves a bonus. The timing of this is very important – the reward has to be given straight after he has performed a behaviour brilliantly. A bonus can consist of extra treats, some titbits that are particularly special, or a game that he really enjoys. This extra bonus is called a 'jackpot' and the effect should be that your dog will work all the harder for you.

WHEN IS A PUNISHMENT A REWARD... OR VICE VERSA?

Most owners think that treats, petting, affection and praise are all suitable rewards for their dogs. In general, we are poor at recognising the effect of our attention – whether positive or negative – on our dogs. You only have to watch the variety of exciting responses from humans when their dogs jump up to see this in action. For example, shouting at your dog, pushing him off or petting him will all have potentially the same effect – and will reward him for doing the very behaviour you didn't want. No wonder the dog does it again.

Punished by rewards

Conversely, despite enjoying their owner's attention, a lot of dogs don't like being cuddled or patted on the head – especially if they are anticipating a different reward, such as a food treat. If you have a tendency to do this to your dog, watch his reaction to it. Does he back away from you slightly? If so, he's trying to tell you that he doesn't really like it.

If you want to stop your dog repeating an annoying behaviour, such as jumping up at people or begging for food, you need to make sure that you are not inadvertently rewarding him for it by giving him attention.

Active ignoring

The opposite of giving attention is ignoring, but ignoring is not passive. Ignoring your dog means turning away from him – facing the other way to avoid eye contact, folding your arms to indicate that you are not going to touch him, and staying silent. Some owners may even need to get up out of their comfortable armchair, march out of the room in an Oscar-winning performance of disgust and close the door behind them – effectively leaving the dog in isolation for a moment or two.

Of course, the effect of human attention on dogs can work in our favour, too – as we can use it to our advantage in training. For this reason, when you are pleased with your dog's behaviour, it's important to tell him so, using eye contact, smiles and friendly body language.

When your dog behaves well, make a fuss of him and let him know you're pleased.

USING CONSEQUENCES IN TRAINING

Not all dogs will respond to training all the time; they have minds of their own, and this makes them so interesting to live with. However, this can sometimes cause problems – both practical and emotional. Dogs rarely 'disobey' for the sake of it – they tend not to follow commands because they don't understand what you want, they are fearful or would rather do something else. In this happens, don't blame your dog but take a hard look at your training methods instead.

If your dog doesn't respond to your commands

1 Ask yourself if there's a reason why he might not be responding. Is he feeling unwell, over-tired, or does he need to relieve himself?

2 Is your motivation sufficient for him to want to work? Does he really like the food, toys, games or treats that you have on offer for him?

No response equals no reward. Consequences can have a powerful effect in dog training.

3 Does he really understand exactly what you are asking him to do? Make it clearer for him.

4 Is he bored, or does he have a competing interest, such as other dogs in the area with whom he would rather be playing?

Consequences, consequences

Bear in mind that our dogs – just like us – can learn that their behaviour can result in consequences. However, these don't have to be frightening or physically confrontational. If your dog doesn't respond to a cue or command that he has previously been taught, then the consequence is that you do not reward him. Instead, turn your back on him and put the treats back in the pot. Being ignored in this way is a powerful message for your dog.

Other consequences might include:

- Taking your dog back into the house rather than continuing on a walk, if he continually pulls on the lead.
- Putting him back on the lead if he doesn't come to you when he is called.
- Gently closing a door in front of him if he's pushing past you to get through it first.

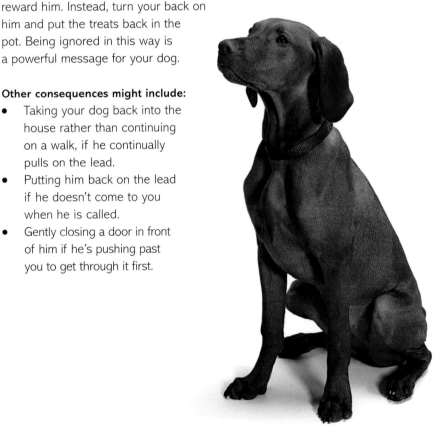

CHAPTER 3
FACTORS AFFECTING LEARNING

We all know how our environment, health and even diet can affect our moods but often overlook the fact that dogs can be just as influenced by these factors – and that it's up to us to control them. The foundations of training must be established in a calm, quiet atmosphere, so you and your dog can focus on each new task without getting distracted. When you have mastered the basics, it's time to start practising out in the big wide world, exposing your dog to the distractions of other dogs, busy areas and noisy situations. It's important to build on success rather than trying to rescue failure.

HEALTH AND DIET

Of course, nobody feels much like learning anything new when they are over-tired or have a headache or upset stomach. The problem is that our dogs cannot tell us these things, and they can end up being labelled as unresponsive or naughty when really they just feel unwell.

You are what you eat

Although it is quite difficult to prove scientifically that certain foods may affect dogs in a variety of ways, anecdotally it seems likely that this is the case. Just as some people cannot eat specific ingredients without feeling unwell, it is possible that some dogs may suffer as a result of a food intolerance or even an allergy. Signs that your dog's diet may not suit him can be very subtle and hard to spot, but the symptoms may have a big impact on his training. Ask your vet for advice if you think that your dog might benefit from a diet change.

Tell-tale symptoms

- Inconsistent digestion: sometimes your dog may experience bouts of diarrhoea or his faeces may be large and smelly.
- He needs to go to the toilet often: five or six times daily shows that

What you put into your dog may well have consequences for his behaviour as well as his overall health.

Clinical problems

If your dog is motivated to train and is happy to be with you, you must consider any possible health reasons if he is ever reluctant to perform a particular exercise. Just a basic sit, for example, can be terribly painful for a dog with hip problems. Always consult your veterinary surgeon if you suspect your dog may have a clinical problem of any kind.

food is not being digested properly or you are over-feeding him.

- He is eating some unusual things, such as sticks, grass, soil, stones, tissues or pieces of paper.
- He exhibits over-excitability or over-activity, lack of concentration, and manic mouthing.
- He has skin irritations, and itching at the base of the tail, feet and belly.
- He has bad breath or flatulence.

Sleepy puppies

Puppies need huge amounts of sleep in order to grow and develop. Sudden tiredness can take owners by surprise. One minute they are running around and the next they are unable to concentrate. Ensure your puppy gets enough sleep.

Exercise affects your dog's mind as well as his body – and it's a joy for him.

UNDER PRESSURE

Just like us, dogs suffer from stress. They cannot tell us when they are feeling under pressure, so we need to learn how to spot the signs (see page 30). Stress has many negative effects on training. Most people couldn't say what they learned on their first driving lesson as stress blocks learning, and, just like us, dogs need to feel secure and comfortable in order to learn new things. The best training is stress-free and enjoyable for both you and your dog.

Old dog, new tricks?

No dog is ever too old to learn. However, older dogs may be anxious about trying out new behaviours, particularly if they have been trained using old-fashioned methods whereby they learned that it was better to do nothing than risk punishment. Old dogs may also be physically slower than younger ones, and may find certain behaviours, such as sitting still, uncomfortable. Young dogs are like sponges – they are always ready and waiting to soak up all the training you can give them. However, hormones can affect adolescent dogs in similar ways to human teenagers.

Just because your dog is enjoying his senior years doesn't mean he won't benefit from learning new things; it can help to give him a new lease of life.

Canine IQ

Is one breed of dog more intelligent than another? This is a difficult question because canine intelligence is simply not the same as ours. Although it might appear that certain breeds learn new tricks and training exercises faster than others, this isn't necessarily a sign of cognitive ability – only a desire to repeat patterns of behaviour. Dogs who run off when they are called, turn a deaf ear when their owners ask them to do something or just act cute so that they don't have to comply with human wishes may be the bright ones after all!

Plan for success

Having a strategic plan for your training may sound much too theoretical but, as with all new skills, you are more likely to achieve long-term success if you have a clear goal at the outset. Plan what you want your dog to learn and imagine how and when you will use this in real life. Then break down the task into tiny stages and teach one chunk at a time. This way, you will see your dog make steady progress towards the end goal. Training in small chunks is far more satisfying and motivating for both of you than trying to do too much, too soon.

No matter what your dog's breed or type, his brain is ready and waiting. It's up to you to channel it in the right direction.

MOVING ON FROM THE PAST

One of the most powerful of all the influences on your dog's attitude to training will be his previous experience of it. Sadly, many dogs are exposed to the 'tell him, make him' school of training, which often involves physical confrontation, fear and punishment. Despite some old-fashioned trainers' assertions, dogs do not constantly engage in conflict between themselves to establish either leadership or hierarchy. Instead, they have many instinctive and learned behaviour patterns that they habitually use to avoid conflict and to maintain harmony within their social group.

Dog training classes

These classes can be a great way of practising your training around other dogs and people. They should always be relaxed and fun – not noisy or chaotic. The training methods that are used should be kind and fair as well as effective, so that both the dogs and owners can enjoy their evening out together.

Good communication

Dogs are great communicators, and their owners need no persuasion to believe this – we know it every time our dogs greet us, we go out for a walk together or we play games. Good training always starts with the spirit of good communication – and clicker training is a perfect starting place for a dog who is unsure about what you, his owner, wants.

Your dog's responses will tell you whether your training methods are right for him. Never be afraid to change them according to his individual needs.

Start with fun in mind

If your dog is a little cautious of training with you – perhaps because he has had some previous bad experiences – or simply because he has never done any training before, begin with an exercise that is fun and easy. The attention exercise (see page 40) and target training (see page 106) are ideal for this.

Your attitude

Gone are the days of 'I say, you do' in dog training. Now, learning is all about good communication and teamwork with your dog. It's no fun if you approach training as a chore, or as a means to suppress your dog's behaviour – it should give him more options for good behaviour.

Listen to your dog

Your dog is always the expert – and he never lies. If he keeps losing concentration during training, walks away from you, or looks bored or unmotivated, he's trying to tell you something. Stop training and take a step back from what you are trying to teach. Are you offering him enough motivation? Is he tired or does he need a break? Are you trying to teach too much at once? Go back to something he knows well, reward this and then review your training methods before your next session.

Your attitudes to training will show in your dog's body language and facial expression. Fun training leads to happy dogs.

UNDERSTANDING YOUR DOG

Despite thousands of years of combined social development, man and dog still have trouble understanding one another from time to time. Although we share many of the same non-verbal expressions of emotion, there are some signals that are totally different in each other's languages, and therefore learning how to 'speak canine' is an essential part of good training for every responsible owner

Read your dog

Look at your dog carefully. You will notice that despite his head shape being so different from yours, there are some remarkable similarities in the facial expression that you will instantly recognise. For example, when we are feeling worried, the muscles in our foreheads pull our eyebrows towards the centre, producing some characteristic 'worry lines'. This expression of anxiety is almost identical in our dogs when they are stressed or worried.

Despite the fact that their physical make-up is so diverse, our dogs also recognise many common human emotional expressions without having to learn them. For example, puppies do not need to learn that a human smile is a good thing, although we are showing our teeth, which is a threat display in dog language. Instead, they know instinctively that it is an expression of pleasure and friendliness.

Learning to read your dog's expressions is an on-going lesson in another language. This dog is eager and ready to respond.

Dog – not man

Despite these similarities, humans sometimes have a tendency to anthropomorphise – attribute human emotions – to their dogs. The most common of these misapprehensions is to say that a dog looks guilty – or that 'he knows he's done wrong' – when in reality he is showing fear and appeasement. This is a particularly unfortunate communication error because we might then assume that the dog will learn from his 'mistake' and, consequently, we are surprised when he repeats the same behaviour that got him into trouble in the first place.

Get to know the signs
Watch your dog carefully and learn to understand his subtle signals that tell you when he's feeling playful, tired, anxious, stressed, unwell or joyful.

Canine expressions are often similar to humans' but it is easy to misread guilt when the dog is really showing appeasement or anxiety. Look at this dog's seemingly 'guilty' expression – ears back, head lowered and heavy brow. She's not being sulky – she just does not know what is being asked of her.

BODY LANGUAGE AND FACIAL EXPRESSIONS

All body language needs to be looked at in context – in other words, the whole dog tells the story, not just one part of it. However, by focusing on various parts of your dog, you can learn to understand some of the expressions that make up canine language.

Ears

Dogs put their ears back when they are feeling anxious – in this instance, they are usually flat to the head. However, they may also put their ears back to show friendliness, in which case, you will often see the inside of each ear.

Eyes

Dogs squint and blink when they are trying to be non-threatening – either because they are being friendly or because they are anxious.

Forehead

Just like humans, dogs furrow their brows when they are worried or when they are focusing intently on something with great concentration. Of course, some breeds, such as Boxers and Shar Peis, have an almost permanently furrowed brow, so this needs to be taken into account by their owners.

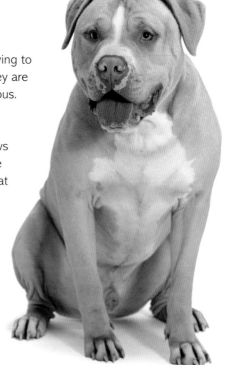

Dogs have a complex set of facial muscles and the ability to show emotion via subtle changes of facial expression – as demonstrated here.

This dog is showing stress – look at the tension in his body, the wide eyes and the ears held right back. He's panting and his facial muscles are tight. 'Get me out of here!'

Tail

Tail wagging means that a dog is happy, doesn't it?
Well, not always. For dogs, tail wagging is as much about disseminating scent information as it is about visual signals, so the speed and position of the tail itself matter, too. Therefore low, fast tail wags nearly always indicate uncertainty in dogs, whereas horizontal, open wags generally demonstrate friendliness. Indeed, some dogs wag so enthusiastically that their tails go round in a 'windmill' style.

Mouth

Most dogs will keep their teeth deliberately concealed when they are being friendly, as this is polite in canine communication. Lip licking and yawning can both be signs of stress, which are worth watching out for in your dog.

Body

Confident dogs carry their weight four-square, while anxious or fearful ones will lower their bodies towards the ground and shift their body weight well away from whatever is worrying them.

CHAPTER 4

TRAINING YOUR DOG

Training dogs has changed dramatically over the past decade, and gone are the days of shouting, forcing your dog into position or using physical strength to make him do what you want. Instead, we rely on the psychology of motivation, encouraging our dogs to be willing team-mates rather than reluctant victims. Animals of all kinds are now trained using positive reinforcement, and clicker training is one of the most effective and enjoyable methods. Based on sound scientific principles, it allows you to communicate with your dog and train him to do practically any action you choose.

CLICKER TRAINING

A clicker is a small plastic box containing a piece of flexible steel. When pressed and released at one end, it makes a distinctive 'click, click' sound. Over a number of repetitions, a dog learns that the sound of the clicker means he's done the right thing and a reward, in the form of food, play or affection, is on its way. The clicker is not a cue or command but a signal of reward (a conditioned reinforcer) that tells the dog why he got the reward. Your dog will make the association between the clicker and treats or toys by repetition and reward. The sound of the clicker marks the dog's action as being right – a little like putting a tick next to a correct sum on a page.

Why is the clicker effective?

The clicker is always positive and highly accurate. Anyone in the family can use it and the message will stay the same. You can give clear information to your dog about his actions up close or from a distance, without your feelings being expressed in your voice. The clicker rewards actions you like – you simply ignore the actions you don't like.

Using a clicker word

Clicker training doesn't have to mean using the actual clicker. Indeed, some exercises are easier without a clicker in your hand, and using a vocal signal to tell the dog when he's got it right is a good alternative. Choose a 'clicker word' with care. It needs to be short, snappy and easy to say. It's also vital that it isn't repeated in your everyday conversation where your dog will learn to ignore it. 'Good', 'Yes', 'Bingo' or 'Wow' are all favourites.

Do I need to use the clicker forever?
It is far easier to teach your dog new exercises using the clicker. However, as soon as he understands an exercise, you no longer need to reward it every time, so you don't have to use the clicker.

Can all dogs be trained using the clicker?

Nearly all dogs, no matter what their age, can be trained with the clicker. Some very nervous dogs may need additional time or help, while older ones who have been trained in 'traditional' ways (we call these 'cross-over' dogs) may be a little reluctant to explore new behaviours at first.

Punishments

All punishments, particularly physical ones, are very old-fashioned, risky, ineffective and, sometimes, cruel. They will always reflect human frustration as well as a lack of imagination. You can adopt a far safer and kinder approach by training your dog without using aversion – after all, we are meant to be the smarter species.

Most dogs work out that the click means that 'a reward is coming' within about four trials. It acts like an interpreter between you and your dog, speeding up training and making it fun.

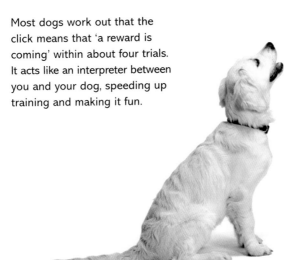

CUES, NOT CORRECTIONS

Clicker training is based on the art of rewards, not punishments. This has many benefits, but the most important is that with each training session you will improve your relationship with your dog.

Problems with punishment

Punishment can be counter-productive but, sadly, many old-fashioned trainers still recommend it as a 'quick fix' for any unwanted behaviour. This is risky because even a 'mild' punishment can have a damaging effect on your dog and his relationship with you.

Teach your dog what you want him to do

Humans are often inclined to try to punish their dogs when they show unwanted behaviour, but the risks of escalated aggression or irresolvable depression are ever-present. Far safer than attempting to stop unwanted behaviour is teaching your dog what you want him to do instead. This transforms a negative situation into a positive one and puts you calmly back in control.

All dogs do things that humans find annoying – your task is to come up with some creative training exercises that teach your dog alternative behaviours that are incompatible with the ones you don't like.

- **Does your dog jump up?** Teach him to sit on cue to greet people politely.
- **Does he pull on the lead?** Train him to walk by your side, targeting your hand as a trick to keep his attention.
- **Is he landscaping your garden by digging holes?** Get him hooked on chewing interactive toys instead.
- **Does he bark?** He cannot bark and hold a soft toy at the same time.

Many dogs think being told off is great sport as they gain eye contact – and your attention.

Although you may need to start out by luring your dog into position using a food treat, very quickly you will be able to phase out using lures.

At this point, a hand signal can still be used to cue your dog into position, but you do not need to hold any food in your hand. Once proficient, many dogs will happily offer you long sequences of behaviours without the need for extra rewards.

WHAT'S MY NAME?

Your dog should always look at you the instant you say his name, wherever you happen to be and whatever distractions are present. This simple act makes the rest of training easy.

1 Start your training in a distraction-free area. Hold a food treat between your thumb and finger and as soon as your dog sniffs at it, lift your hand so that it is between your eyes.

2 Click or say 'Good' and immediately reward him for looking towards your face. Repeat this four times.

3 On the fifth go, say your dog's name in a cheerful voice. Keep your hand still by your side. If he looks at your face, click or say 'Good' and then give him a tasty reward. If he is reluctant, then bring your hand towards your face to help him.

4 Repeat this pattern four or five times, rewarding when your dog looks at your face.

Without a treat

Now, without any food in your hand, ask your dog for his attention by saying his name. The instant he looks up at your face, you can click and reward him generously from a pot or pouch. Repeat this action until it's perfect.

Many dogs probably think their name is 'No!' Make sure yours associates his name with good things.

Change your position

It's time to move your body position. If you have been sitting down, stand and repeat the exercise. If you have been standing up, then sit down and try again. You can try practising this in a different room or location, too. This will help to 'generalise' the behaviour, so your dog understands that he should look at you whenever you say his name, regardless of the location or any distractions.

Moving on
Say your dog's name when you are around the house and out in the garden, even when he's distracted. Always click or say 'Good' when he looks at you in response and give a treat or game. Dogs quickly learn to ignore their owners if they simply repeat their names and fail to give them rewards.

Gradually build up your training sessions until you are able to get your dog's eye contact in even the most distracting of situations, such as off lead in the park.

FoLLoW FooD IN THE HAND

Although it might sound strange, many dogs, particularly puppies, just don't know how to follow food. This is important because using a food lure in your hand allows your dog to be manoeuvred into the desired position without you having to push or pull him.

1 Hold a small piece of really tasty food in between your thumb and your forefinger. You should let your dog see, smell and even taste it, but do not let him snatch it out of your fingers.

2 Move the food around slowly, at your dog's head height, and encourage him to follow it. Click and give him the treat if he moves with you and keeps his nose on the food as you move your hand around.

Most dogs have no problem following a food lure if held correctly between the fingers – see if you can get your dog to follow it in a circular motion.

Trouble shooting

Polite dogs can sometimes be a little over-cautious when they are following a food lure. This can happen if you move your hand away too quickly at the outset. Sensitive dogs perceive that you are trying to keep the food to yourself and they may back away politely. So start out by moving the food slowly and make sure that you give your dog lots of praise and encouragement for following it.

Food on the floor
Once your dog is happily following food in your hand, you can move on to teaching him to follow food as it rolls along the floor. This will be a useful addition to your training 'toolkit' later.

'Muggers', on the other hand, are those dogs that are just a little too keen. If your dog tries to snatch the treat out of your fingers, he needs to learn some self-control. Use a lower-grade food, which is less tempting, and keep it well tucked into your hand so that he cannot be rewarded accidentally for grabbing. Move the food only 2.5cm (1in) or so when practising, click and treat when your dog is gentle, and never give the food if he is being rough.

If your dog has problems following a food lure, then go back a couple of stages and make it easier for him. He just needs more practice.

'SIT'

There are at least 101 things that your dog cannot do if he's sitting. Teaching the sit is easy and it also instils some impulse control at the same time.

> ### From lure to reward
> **Using a food lure is very useful for kick-starting your training but once your dog has got the hang of moving into the right position, you need to stop using the lure as quickly as possible. This prevents reliance on the food.**

1 Show your dog a food treat. Hold it tightly between your finger and thumb, so that he can smell it and even taste it but can't steal it from you.

2 Position the treat close to his nose. Slowly lift your hand up and back, so that he has to look right up in order to follow your fingers.

3 This causes a physical chain reaction – as he raises his head, his rear end has to go down. The instant his bottom hits the ground, click or say 'Good' and give him the treat. Bear in mind that the click ends the behaviour. Repeat this action at least five times.

4 Now repeat the movement again, but this time say the word 'Sit' just before you move the food lure.

Without the lure

1 Keep your hand in exactly the same position as previously, but this time don't hold any food in it.

2 Ask your dog to sit. If he does so, click or say 'Good' immediately, then give him a food treat from your other hand, or from a pot or pouch.

Note: If your dog does not sit when asked, go back to having a food lure in your hand and practise a few more times before trying without the lure.

1

2

3

Sit homework
Practise getting your dog to respond to the word 'Sit' before he gets anything he likes – his dinner, putting his lead on, or being let out into the garden. Ask him to sit in different positions, too – for, example, by your side as well as in front of you.

TAKE THE 'SIT' FURTHER

Once your dog understands that your hand signal or the command 'Sit' means that he should park his bottom, the time has come for you to take this exercise further and teach him the next steps.

Sitting next to your heel

Most dogs learn that 'Sit' means 'sit opposite your owner'. This is fine, but it may be that you have ambitions to do competition obedience with your dog, or simply that you want to have him sit next to you at the kerb when you cross the road. Here's how to teach him to sit beside you.

1 Lure your dog with a food treat to sit next to your left heel. Click and treat him. If he sits very crooked, or a long way from your leg, you can position him next to a wall, so that he is guided easily into getting it right.

2 Practise this at least 10 times, luring him with a treat just to get him into the correct position.

3 Next, remove the food from your hand. Ask your dog to assume the position by your leg, then click and get a treat to give to him. This transforms the lure into a reward.

Sit at heel: the basis of competitive obedience training and useful manners.

Sit and stay

As soon as your dog has mastered the movement required to sit, you need to teach him to sit still.

1 Start off by asking your dog to sit in the usual way.

2 Count three seconds, then click and throw the treat, as this moves him out of the position.

3 Repeat the exercise, but ask for seven seconds before clicking and giving your dog a treat.

4 Ask your dog to sit for random amounts of time. The click always ends the behaviour.

Try to keep your body language and facial expression relaxed while training the stay – your dog may become anxious if you are stiff and tense.

'SIT' TROUBLE SHOOTING

Urban myths abound in dog training and one of them is that breeds such as Greyhounds, Whippets and Lurchers cannot be taught to sit, but this is simply not true. While these breeds may not find it hugely comfortable to sit on a hard floor, they can certainly position themselves into a sit, given the right motivation and good training.

COMMON PROBLEMS WITH TEACHING 'SIT'	SOLUTION
Your dog's front legs come off the ground, or he jumps up to try to get the food.	Your hand is too high. Lower it so that it is at the same height as your dog's nose when he's standing, then move it in such a way that he has to tip his head backwards.
Your dog is bored or looking away.	Dogs really do tell you what they think of your training! Are you repeating 'Sit, sit, sit, SIT'? If so, go back to luring with food for a while to get success. Try a better treat or move to a quieter area. Keep sessions short and fun.
Your dog seems to have trouble sitting.	Go back to the attention exercise, so your dog has to look directly up at your face. Check that he is in good physical health and not uncomfortable in any way. Just occasionally, a reluctance to sit can indicate that something else is wrong.

Tips for sight hounds

- Provide your dog with a comfortable sitting place – he's got a bony bottom after all. A furry mat or a doggie duvet can be just the thing.
- Move your hand ultra slowly when luring him, so that he has time to adjust to the position.
- Catch your dog 'in the act' of sitting and click and treat him when he does.
- Teach your hound to lie down first, and then teach him to sit up from the down position. This training method works a treat for reluctant sitters of all breeds and types.

This beautiful Lurcher proves that sitting is possible for all breeds of dog – but comfort is everything.

Tiny breeds

The smaller your dog, the more accurate your hand position will need to be when you are teaching the sit on cue. Just concentrate on moving your hand only a tiny bit at a time, and click and treat your dog for making moves in the right direction, such as tilting his head up. Use tiny treats so that you can be generous without filling your little dog up too fast.

'DOWN'

There's nothing more impressive than saying 'Down' in a quiet voice and watching your dog hit the deck with speed and enthusiasm. It's not difficult to achieve and here's how you can teach him.

1 With your dog sitting, hold a food lure close to his nose. Lower your hand very slowly to the floor, directly between his front paws. Hang on to the treat by turning your palm down, with the food hidden inside your hand.

2 You will soon be able to tell if your dog is trying if his front end goes down in a bowing position, or if he moves backwards slightly. Both these things mean you just have to wait. Don't be tempted to move your hand along the floor, as this will lure the dog back into a standing position.

3 Be patient – if your dog loses interest, just show him the treat and then lure him towards the floor, before turning your hand palm down, so that the treat is hidden.

4 The instant your dog lies down, click or say your clicker word, then drop the treat on to the floor between his front paws and let him eat it. (This prevents him following your hand back up again like a yo-yo.)

5 Repeat several times, sometimes with the food in your hand, sometimes without. Still click and put a treat on the floor after your dog has moved into the down position. Once you can guarantee he will lie down by following your hand to the floor, say the word 'Down' just before moving the lure.

Down on command

After having lured your dog a few times with your hand, stand up and tuck the food treat behind your back. Give one quiet cue: 'Down'. As he has just accomplished several downs in a row, this is the behaviour he is most likely to try in order to get the click and treat. As long as he is still engaged with you, be patient and wait. Keep your eye on him: the instant he lies down, be ready to click and give him a jackpot of treats to reinforce the behaviour.

DOWN STAY

Once your dog has learned to lie down on command, you can then teach him to stay in that position for longer, by waiting before you click and treat. Build this up from just five seconds to 90 seconds, over several training sessions, keeping your dog in position for random amounts of time. Praise him all the time he is lying down. The click ends the behaviour, so make sure that you click while he is still lying down, then treat two to three seconds later.

The art of staying still is difficult for most dogs and it needs to be practised in many different environments – in the park, countryside, house and garden.

Stay with distractions

Now it's time to add some distractions to the 'Down' exercise. These need to be relatively gentle initially – if your dog moves, you will know that you have done too much too soon. If this happens, just go back to a simpler task and build up the distractions once again until you achieve success.

1 With your dog lying down, take two paces away from him. Then move back to him, praise him and click and treat.

2 Ask your dog to lie down and clap your hands in front of you. If he stays in position, click and treat him.

3 Keep him lying down in one place while you take off one shoe and then put it back on again.

4 Ask him to lie down, then sit in your favourite armchair while you count to 30. Return to him before clicking and giving him a treat.

5 Build up to being able to walk all around your dog while he stays in position. Do this in small stages.

Build up the distractions gradually – and change only one of the criteria, such as the duration or movement, at a time.

DOWN: TROUBLE SHOOTING

Sometimes it can be difficult to encourage small or rather anxious dogs to go into the down position just by using a tasty food lure. In these instances, a prop can be helpful: try either a low coffee table or a chair with a low base, or sit on the floor and use your leg as a bridge. Luring your dog under the prop helps to establish the physical movement that is necessary for 'Down'. This will train his body while his mind catches up.

COMMON PROBLEMS WITH TEACHING 'DOWN'	SOLUTION
Dog keeps standing up.	Your hand position is incorrect. Most likely, it is too far away from your dog's front paws. Try putting the treat on the floor straight between his paws or slightly towards his chest.
Dog is not following food to the floor.	Your hand may be moving too fast. Think about moving your hand in slow motion.
Dog puts front end down but his bottom stays in the air.	Just wait and be patient. Your dog's bottom will sink down on to the floor eventually.
Dog lies down but stands straight back up again.	That food reward must be repeatedly released onto the floor – otherwise your dog will follow your hand up and down like a jack-in-the-box.

1 Sit down on the floor with one leg outstretched in front of you. Bend your knee so that it forms a bridge.

2 Lure your dog under your leg with the food treat. Most dogs find this easiest if you put the treat on the floor, just out of reach.

3 You will see that the first good efforts involve just his front end going down, so that his chest is on the floor. Click and give your dog the treat for making this effort.

4 Repeat the exercise, but this time see if you can hold out and only click and treat your dog for a full-body down.

5 Once your dog has repeated the behaviour of lying down under your leg four or five times, he's ready to try it without the bridge. Stay in the same position but lure him just next to your leg rather than under it. Now you can phase out the food lure and add the cue.

Teaching the down needs a little more patience than the sit position, but be persistent.

SETTLE DOWN

The settle down is not a formal stay. Instead, it is a 'relax' command, which tells your dog to simply be calm and settled. This is one of the most useful commands in your training repertoire. It's ideal when waiting in the vet's surgery, for when visitors arrive at home, or when you're in a café with friends. Moreover, teaching the settle down couldn't be easier because you can do most of your practice at home, sitting comfortably in an armchair.

1 With your dog on a collar and lead, take him into the room where you are going to settle for a while and then sit down.

2 Put the end of his lead firmly under one foot, giving him enough slack in the lead so that he can stand up, turn round and lie down comfortably.

3 In a quiet voice, say 'Settle'. Now wait. Do not talk to your dog, look at him or touch him. At this point, some dogs attempt to get attention by barking, straining on the lead, chewing it, or even getting tangled up in it. You must ignore all of these strategies completely.

4 Eventually, your dog will lie down. At this stage, you can quietly pet and praise him, but try not to excite him again.

5 After about three or four minutes, say 'Finish'. Get up quietly and remove your dog's lead.

Teaching your dog to simply relax and do nothing is perhaps the most useful of all your commands – especially in social situations.

Practising the settle down requires some arm-chair dog training on your part.

Training tip

This exercise needs to be practised every day for at least a week. It's perfect to practise in the evenings when you sit down to watch some television or to quietly read a book or newspaper.

After only a few days you will notice that your dog settles down more quickly when you ask him to do so. At this stage, it is sensible to take the exercise a little further and to practise the routine in different rooms in the house, and then in other locations.

Clicker training is beneficial

Interestingly, clicker training may also have implications for us, as trainers. Ask most clicker trainers how they feel about training their dog with the clicker and they love it. As the tool is always associated with positive events, it is possible that humans as well as dogs build up associated pleasurable responses to seeing, holding and using the clicker. This may help to 'anchor' a positive emotional state in not only the dog but also his human owner.

COME WHEN CALLED

Teaching your dog to come when he's called means that he will be able to have more freedom where it is safe to give him off-lead exercise. It's essential for basic safety that your dog is trained to come straight to you every time you call him.

1 Standing or crouching only a couple of steps away from your dog, call him in a friendly voice.

2 Waggle a tasty food lure in your outstretched hand and then start moving backwards, making sure that your body language is really encouraging for your dog.

> ## Caution!
> **Never call your dog to you and then do something unpleasant, such as flea spraying or giving medical treatments. He's likely to view this as a punishment for coming when called.**

3 If he shows no response, clap your hands or make silly noises until he comes towards you. The instant that he does so, click or say 'Good' and then give him several treats straight away – do this by putting them on the floor in front of you.

4 Gradually increase the distance he has to come to get the food, making sure you praise him and give him delicious rewards and a game with a toy for coming when you call him.

> ## Move away
> **Always try to move away from your dog when you call him. It might be very tempting to move towards him if he does not come, but then who is doing the recall?**

5 Now practise calling your dog to you at unusual moments in and around the house, and then outside in the garden or yard. Build up his recall before you practise in the park or woods where there are distractions.

Make sure you use open, welcoming body language to call your dog to you. Encourage him all the time, so that he knows he's doing the right thing.

As soon as your dog comes to you, click or say your clicker word and then put down a small jackpot of treats on the floor for your dog to eat. You can then hold him gently by the collar.

RECALL BOOMERANG AND SPEED GAMES

You can add speed to your dog's recalls by playing these exciting games together. They also have the benefit of making your training sessions fun and more enjoyable for both of you.

Recall boomerang

This game requires two or more people, a clicker and some delicious food treats to motivate the dog and reward good behaviour.

1 Two (or more) people stand or crouch down opposite each other, holding 10 food treats each.

2 The first person calls the dog. As soon as he comes, they click and put two treats on the ground in front of them for him to eat.

3 The next person now calls the dog and does the same thing when the dog runs to them.

4 The first person calls again. This time, when the dog comes back to them, the person clicks and then lightly touches the dog's collar before allowing him to eat the treats. This gets the dog accustomed to having his collar held when he returns on command.

Teach your dog to be a canine boomerang by zooming backwards and forwards between you and a friend, taking it in turns to call him.

Food circuits

This fast and furious game transforms food into a chase toy. Most dogs love running – it's highly rewarding – so throwing food for your dog to run after and then eat offers a perfect combination of rewards.

1 Start by showing your dog a medium-sized piece of food – ideally, it should be about the size of your fingernail.

2 Throw it a short distance – only a metre or so – low along the floor, so that it rolls away from your dog.

3 Allow him to trot out and eat the food morsel and then call him back to you for another go.

4 On his return, make sure he comes up to you, and then lure him around your back before you throw the food out again.

5 Gradually build up the distance, so that your dog can happily follow the food and chase out after it, getting progressively faster. This is a great reward for coming when he is called.

Encourage your dog to chase out after the treat that you have thrown.

Then encourage him back, lure him round your legs and throw the treat again.

RECALL WITH DISTRACTIONS

Calling your dog to you when you are outdoors and competing with a wide range of wonderful smells, sights and sounds can be quite a challenge. In these circumstances, there are three rules that you always need to observe in order to ensure reliable recalls.

Be more exciting than the environment

This means putting your mobile phone away and paying attention to your dog. Play games with him on walks by taking one special toy that he never sees at any other time. Entice him to track scent trails that you have laid (see page 102), so that you are effectively 'hunting' together, and make sure you are armed with treats so tasty that he won't even think about ignoring you.

Manage the situation so you don't let him fail

If your dog has a wandering eye and selective hearing, then it's up to you to manage the situation so he doesn't end up rewarding himself for running off. Management may seem dull, but some short-term control can lead to long-term freedom. Teach him to check in with you frequently, and use a long line or extending lead if you are unsure as to how he will respond to your call you are when out and about together (see page 64).

Times not to call your dog

Bear in mind that each and every time you call your dog to you and he does not respond, it is another nail in your prompt recall coffin. During these times, it is better to remain silent and wait, or even to walk away from him. As soon as he looks towards you, or moves away from the distraction, call and reward him for good responses. Of course, in the case of an emergency, you will call your dog no matter what the other distractions may happen to be.

> **Delayed reactions**
> Never ever scold your dog for taking too long to come to you – this will only put him off returning to you next time.

When not to call your dog…

- When he's in the act of going to the toilet.
- When you need to do something less than pleasant to him, such as nail clipping or spraying him for fleas.
- When he's greeting another dog.
- When he's letting off a huge burst of energy.
- When you know that you haven't got a hope of him coming back to you.

You'll need to use top-class rewards when calling your dog past other dogs.

RECALL: TROUBLE SHOOTING

It's a sensible strategy to use a long line if you are unsure how your dog will respond on the first few occasions outdoors, but it should be used only as a back-up tool and not as a means to reel him towards you or pull him. A line can be made of any lightweight cord or tape, as long as it is strong and attached to your dog's collar with a safe trigger clasp. Most long lines are between 5m (16ft) and 12m (39ft).

1 When you get to a safe area outside, clip the long line to your dog's collar and then unclip his usual lead. This establishes a routine.

2 Before allowing him any freedom, ask him to give you attention and eye contact by saying his name. Click and treat for this.

3 Allow your dog only about 2m (6½ft) of freedom, then wait for a good opportunity to call his name and reward him for coming, even though it's only a short distance.

4 Gradually allow him more length on the line. Recall him frequently and click and treat and play wonderful games with your special toy with him.

5 When you are confident that he will come when called, allow the line to drag on the floor behind your dog. This gives you a safety line to fall back on.

Note: With your dog on a long line, it's essential that you continue the same routine you used with your previous recall training.

Special toys

Play with your dog with his new toy inside on several occasions, but always put it away after a really good game, so that he's left wanting more. After several games with this toy, your dog should be very keen to play with it and will be amazed when you suddenly produce it from your pocket when you're out on a walk.

A long-line should only ever be used attached to an ordinary collar, and with care.

Outside rewards

Although most dogs respond well to food treats when they are inside and have little to distract them, when you are outside you may find that your dog's attention is being side-tracked. If this happens, you may need to up-grade your training by getting him addicted to playing with a special toy instead. Suitable toys are tuggies and balls on ropes – these allow the toy to be thrown with ease but have a handle you can hold onto.

Top tip

Call your dog to you frequently when you're out on walks, and reward him generously for coming, then let him run free again immediately. Many dogs think that coming back when they are called will result in being put on the lead and taken home.

Training Your Dog   65

'STAND'

Teaching a stand can be very useful, especially for visits to the vet and when grooming your dog. It also means that you can dry his feet easily with a towel without having a battle.

1 With your dog in a sit position, hold a food treat right in front of his nose. Now move your hand away slowly, parallel to the floor, at his head height. (This is difficult for humans; we think of stand as being a vertical position, whereas for a dog it requires a horizontal movement.)

2 As soon as your dog moves forwards into a stand position, click or say 'Good' and give him the treat.

3 Practise this exercise until your dog is confident in just following your hand without the treat in it.

4 At this stage you can add the cue word 'Stand' just before he moves into position.

Lure your dog from a sit position into a stand by moving the treat parallel to the floor at your dog's head height.

From the down position

1 With your dog in the down, hold a food treat close to his nose and bring your hand in an inverted 'L' shape – vertically upwards and then horizontally outwards.

2 Move your hand slowly so that he can follow it. As soon as he's on his feet, click and release the treat.

Trouble shooting
If your dog lies down, your hand is too low. If he jumps up, it is probably too high. If he walks more than one step forward, you are moving the treat too far and too fast.

Showing off
It used to be thought that show dogs shouldn't be taught the sit or down positions as only a stand is required in the conformation ring but trained dogs can easily distinguish between the taught positions. Teaching a combination of sit, stand, down really helps them to understand which position matches which cue, making the exercises more reliable.

Your hand needs to move in an 'inverted L' shape to encourage a stand from the down.

WALKING ON A LOOSE LEAD

The main reason why so many dogs pull on the lead is that they get rewarded for it! Dogs work out that by pulling they get to the park more quickly and can lead their owners wherever they want to go, rather than the other way round. It is imperative that you start your dog's lead training in a calm, quiet place, not when you are trying to get to the park in the rain. Training your dog to walk by your side takes patience, time and persistence, and many people find this difficult because they don't put in enough practice. If your dog never goes out on the lead, you cannot expect him to know how to behave on it.

In the right place

Dogs need information about when they are in the right place when walking nicely on the lead, and this is where the clicker really comes into its own. Rather than telling your dog off for pulling, take away all his fun by standing still. When he is in the right place, let him know by clicking and treating, and then moving forwards.

You can choose which side your dog should walk when on lead – but be consistent or he will try to cross in front of you while walking.

Beware! If you allow your puppy to pull you when you're out walking on the lead when he's tiny, he will do it for life. Don't allow bad habits to develop.

Decide which side

It is only conventional obedience training that dictates we should walk our dogs on the left-hand side. For ease of training in the initial stages, pick the side on which you prefer to walk your dog on and stick with it.

Habit forming

If you have a puppy, make sure you never let him get into the habit of pulling on the lead. Think of the lead as a thin strand of cotton, so you don't rely on it to drag him along. Never follow your puppy but always make sure that he follows you instead.

BEFORE YOU START

Produce a lead and most dogs think that something fun is going to happen. Indeed, many will immediately start acting like uncontrolled hooligans, bouncing and leaping around in anticipation of going out for a walk. If your dog acts like this and you clip on the lead, guess what? You've rewarded him for the behaviour you don't like.

Before you start

Produce your dog's lead and ask him to sit. If he does so, click and give him a treat, and then clip his lead on. This helps to reinforce the idea that calm, quiet behaviour gets rewards. On the other hand, if he starts to bark, leap around, jump up, or becomes over-excited in any other way, simply say 'Too bad', and then put the lead away again. For most dogs, this comes as a bit of a surprise, but be warned – one trial is not enough.

A simple head-collar acts like power-steering for dogs, and prevents pulling.

Wait until your dog calms down, then go through the same process again. After a few repetitions, he will work out that his behaviour causes the lead to be put away. As soon as you see signs that he is trying to control his excitement, ask him to sit, and click and treat him if he does so.

Comfort first

All dogs need to wear a comfortable collar for walking, and the wider and more padded it is, the better. Choke chains, prong collars and other pieces of punitive equipment are outdated and cruel, and should never be used. If your dog is an expert puller, a head-collar can put you gently back in control, allowing you to exercise him whilst working on his re-training.

Teach your dog to put on his own head-collar, using treats and working in small stages – this helps him to accept it.

No lead jerks
Dogs have sensitive necks. They have nerves and muscles that can easily be damaged by rough lead jerks, dragging or pulling. Many dogs pull away from their owners because they have learned that being on the lead is painful – and they are simply trying to get away from it.

GETTING STARTED

It may seem rather odd, but the best way to begin training, or re-training, your dog to walk nicely on the lead is to start by standing still. This is because taking even one single step in the direction that the dog wants to go will reward him for pulling.

Lesson one

1 Start off by putting your dog on the lead in the sitting room, kitchen, hallway or garden. Stand still. Hold the lead close to your body to prevent your hand being pulled towards him.

2 Hold a tasty food treat in the hand closest to your dog. Let him know it's there. As soon as he puts slack in the lead and looks at you, click or say 'Good' and then give him the treat by dropping it close to your heel.

3 Turn slightly on the spot, so your body moves a little but your feet stay still. Your dog will have to take a step or two to keep next to your side. Watch his position – if there is any tension in the lead, stand still and wait, making sure the hand holding the lead stays in place.

Walking politely on the lead is all about your dog understanding that he'll get rewards for being next to you – and that any tension on the lead results in you standing still.

4 Every time there's some slack in the lead, just click or say 'Good' and give your dog a food treat to reward him for his behaviour. Do this by placing it beside your heel.

5 Repeat this exercise several times and then stop and have an enjoyable game together. Be generous with the food treats initially, as lead training can be perceived as rather dull by your dog at the outset.

Challenge

Place five cones in a line (or you can use your dining room furniture to create a mini slalom). Weave in and out of the obstacles, keeping the dog's lead slack the whole time. At the end of the line, turn 360 degrees and then go back through the obstacles again.

Take the five-cone challenge. Can you slalom through the cones, and then back again, without your dog putting any tension on the lead?

Lesson two

Once your dog has started to understand that slack in the lead means good things when you are standing still, the next stage is to get him to comply when you are both moving.

1 Start off by standing still as you did in lesson one with your dog on the lead standing beside you (see pages 72–73).

2 Keep your dog's attention, and take one or two steps. Click when you see a 'J' in the lead, and then drop the food treat for him to eat.

3 Set off again – this time three steps – always watching for the slack lead that gets rewards and standing still as soon as there is any tension. At this stage, some dogs try to use their strength, body weight, or low centre of gravity to pull you off balance. Keep the hand holding the lead tucked into your waist band to prevent this.

4 Repeat this exercise, just taking a few steps at a time and clicking and giving your dog treats for a slack lead.

Note: Keep the training session short and sweet and always stop after only about five repetitions.

> ### Top tip
> Dropping the treat on the floor for your dog to eat prevents snatching, and also encourages him to focus on the floor, rather than your hands.

Always make sure that you keep your dog's attention while you're walking and click for a slack lead.

5 In this session you are going to repeat walking for a few paces and giving clicks and treats, but you are also going to change direction and then see if you can keep your dog walking with you.

Note: Remember that the lead should not be tight – even when you turn around. Once you are confident with this exercise, change the environment in which you are practising, but keep it relatively calm. Perhaps use a hallway, the garden or a quiet stretch of path.

As soon as your dog walks ahead of you, stand still. Keep the hand holding the lead tucked into your body.

Stay still until he puts himself back into the correct position with slack in the lead – click and treat or move off again.

TAKING IT OUTDOORS

When your lead-work training indoors and in the garden is reliable, you can begin practising outside on walks. Don't expect too much too soon. Initially, you may stand still more than you walk forward, but be patient. You can still reinforce your dog for perfect lead-walking with clicks and treats, but for most dogs the action of being allowed to move forward soon becomes rewarding in itself.

Training walks

The walks you take your dog on in training should be carefully planned and managed. Avoid those where your dog knows the route and anticipates a free run at the end of it – or his excitement may over-ride your training to date. Equally, be sensitive to his needs and don't walk him past gateways where

Make walking on lead part of your training schedule, rather than just for exercise.

Remember to give your dog plenty of verbal encouragement and click and treat frequently for a slack lead.

The advanced version of heelwork: practise walking with your dog by your side in a safe area, off lead.

other dogs fence-run and bark – this can be quite an ordeal, and most dogs are likely to want to pull to get past as quickly as possible. The ideal training walk is one that leads nowhere in particular and is not too tempting in terms of interesting smells and the distractions of other dogs. This allows you both to concentrate on actual training rather than exercising or socialising. My favourite training walk is round the block, or to the post box and back.

Head-collars

If you're in a hurry or your dog is very strong and well practised at pulling on the lead, a head-collar can be the answer (see page 70). This acts like power steering and is kind and effective. Some dogs find them restrictive, so click and treat when your dog is in the right place, as this will hasten your training.

Training Your Dog   77

TROUBLE SHOOTING: WALKING ON A LEAD

Teaching your dog to walk nicely on the lead takes time and patience, and it is only achieved if you practise it in the same way as other training exercises. Bear in mind that pulling on lead is rewarding for dogs. They get to their destination faster and, if allowed, by their chosen route. Always ensure you decide where to go, at what pace, and when you stop, not your dog! For this reason, use an extending lead only to give extra freedom in the park, not for walking at heel.

Extending leads are the enemy of good lead-walking unless you use them strategically.

COMMON PROBLEMS WITH LEAD TRAINING	SOLUTION
Dog jumps up to get the food.	Keep the food out of sight, such as in a pocket, or tuck your hand up on your hip. Make the click or the signal 'Good' do the work for you.
Dog lowers his body to the ground and tries to pull you along.	Some dogs are so expert at pulling on the lead that they know all the tricks in the book! If your dog is really well practised, then using a head-collar is a wise move. After all, you would not expect to take a horse for a walk on only a thin piece of string.
Dog is too distracted by the environment to concentrate on lead-walking training.	This is a common problem for puppies or young dogs that have not experienced very much of the world. It is too much to expect them to cope with thinking about lead walking at the same time as assimilating all the sights, sounds and smells going on around them. Make sure that your dog gets lots of exposure to the environment by taking him out on a body harness. This will not stop him from pulling, but it does prevent it from becoming worse. Continue to practise your lead walking indoors and in quiet areas where he can concentrate, so that you can put this into practice once he has grown in confidence.
Dog refuses to walk!	This is pulling on the lead in reverse. Sometimes it is a symptom that your dog is fearful or anxious outside. On other occasions, it can be because he has learned to pull on the lead away from you. Give him lots of rewards for heading in the right direction, even if only for a few paces.

'LEAVE IT'

Dogs explore the world by picking things up with their mouths to check how they taste and feel. They also steal items for attention. Teaching your dog not to touch things can be a real life-saver, as well as saving your sanity. To teach him the 'Leave' command, make sure you are somewhere calm and quiet. This is an exercise that requires concentration from both of you at the outset.

1 Hold a tasty treat in your hand, and close your fingers around it tightly. Present your hand to your dog and wait patiently while he sniffs, licks and nibbles, trying to get the food.

2 Keep your hand still – do not be tempted to pull it away from your dog. Stay quiet – it's important that you do not say anything.

3 Watch carefully. As soon as your dog takes his nose away from your hand, even for a split second, click, or say 'Good', then release the treat.

4 Repeat this several times. Remember to click and give a treat every time you see daylight between your dog's muzzle and your hand. Most dogs learn this incredibly quickly – usually in four to six repetitions.

5 Now wait until your dog has taken his nose away from your hand for the count of three, then click and treat. At this stage, lots of dogs will turn their face away as if to resist temptation. If you see this happening, click and treat immediately.

> **Adults only**
> This exercise must always be initiated by an adult. Once the basics have been taught, children can take over. Dogs' teeth, even in puppies, can be hard and sharp, so safety comes first.

When starting out with the 'Leave it'
exercise, make sure you keep the hand
containing the food completely still –
resting it against your knee is helpful.

Watch your dog carefully – as soon
as he takes his nose and mouth away
from your hand, click and give him
a treat with your other hand.

MOVING ON TO OPEN HAND

The next stage is to take the training further, so you are using an open hand, and then to add a cue. Here's how you do it.

1 With the food still closed in your hand, build up the amount of time that your dog will wait with his nose well away from your hand to about 10 seconds. Keep on practising until this is perfect, and at least four times.

> ### Stay in control
> Once you click or say 'Good', always give your dog the piece of food by taking it from your palm and offering it with your other hand. This will prevent him thinking that he can just help himself – even after you have clicked.

2 At this point you can add in the command 'Leave'. Say this in a calm, quiet voice, not a threatening one. You need to say the word before you move your hand down to your dog's eye level.

3 Once your dog has got the hang of this, repeat the exercise, but this time say 'Leave', and then present the food on your open hand.

4 If your dog tries to take the food from your open palm, simply close your fingers around it again. Do not jerk your hand away. This is very important as it is likely to encourage some dogs to snatch.

5 Click and treat your dog for moving away from the food, as you did before, even though he can see it.

6 Gradually build up the time that your dog keeps his nose away from the food once you have given him the command to leave. See if you can get him to wait for 10 seconds before you click and reward.

Once your dog is reliably taking his nose away from your closed hand, you can try opening it so that he can see the food as well as smell it – he must not touch!

If your dog does come forward to try and take the food, simply close your hand so that you conceal it once more. Be careful not to snatch your hand away or this may cause him to grab.

TROUBLE SHOOTING: LEAVE IT

Most dogs learn the foundations of the leave exercise incredibly fast. If taught using these methods, they rapidly understand that it is their own behaviour that is controlling when they get the food or item – and when they don't. However, bear in mind that dogs are born to be scavengers – and to reward themselves whenever possible. This means that if they are given an opportunity to eat or take something that they want, they will always do so.

Wear a glove

Some dogs – particularly those that are adolescent or have not yet learned to control their own impulses – can be very persistent at trying to get the food from your hand when first learning this exercise. Ironically, these are the very dogs that benefit most from increasing their self control, so don't give up. Use a glove to protect your hand if your dog is scratching you or using his teeth on your skin to try to get you to release the food. Train in very short sessions, and be careful with your timing – it's essential that you click as your dog moves away from the food in your hand, not as he is approaching it.

Keep calm and quiet while teaching the 'Leave' exercise; your dog needs to focus.

COMMON PROBLEMS WITH TEACHING LEAVE	SOLUTION
Dog bites or scratches at your hand, and it hurts.	If your dog is biting really hard at your hand to try and get the food, you can wear a glove initially to protect your skin. Dogs that tend to be rough are prime candidates for this exercise as they need to learn how to control their paws and teeth, so be persistent.
Dog backs off straight away.	Perfect! It may be that your dog has good manners and worked out that he must not touch the food in one trial. Continue with the more advanced version of this exercise.
Dog barks at you.	Some dogs will try other strategies to get the food once they realise that they cannot simply take it from your hand. Polite ones sit or lie down. Less polite dogs may bark at you, paw at you with their claws, or try to sneak round the back of your chair to reach your hand in the hope that you won't see them. Ignore all this creative behaviour. Always be vigilant and make sure that your dog never gets the food except by backing away from it.
Dog backs off but then tries to come forward to snatch at the food.	This is a timing issue. Make sure that you click and release the treat only when your dog is taking his nose off your hand or is backing away slightly. The food reward must never be given if your dog comes forward to take it.

TAKE IT TWO STEPS FURTHER

Most dogs learn the basics of the 'Leave it' exercise within minutes. However, it is sensible to consolidate what your dog has learned by increasing the amount of time he will resist the food, and by asking him to leave even when the treat is not in your hand. Practise one of the following exercises every day for speedy results.

Duration, duration, duration

1 Start off by asking your dog to leave the food on your open palm for a count of five. Click and treat.

2 Now take the exercise a step further and ask your dog to leave the food for a count of 25. Click and treat.

3 The next step is to repeat the action, this time leaving the food for a count of seven and clicking and treating as before.

4 It's the big one. If your dog has been successful on the previous three occasions, ask him to leave for a count of 45 seconds. Click and give more than one treat if he manages this, and let him know you are really pleased with him.

Once your dog masters the basics of the leave, increase the time he doesn't touch – work up to 45 seconds in small stages.

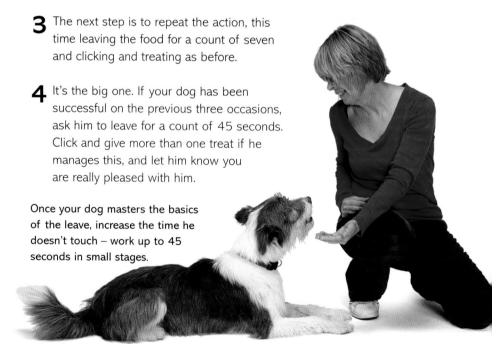

Location, location, location

Dogs learn to respect the food you hold in your hands, but many think food on the floor or in easy-to-reach places is theirs, so this may take more practice.

1 Ask your dog to 'Leave it'. Place a piece of food on a chair and guard it with your cupped hand in such a way that if he comes forward to take it you are ready to cover it with your hand.

2 As soon as he has backed off, you can click, pick up the treat and give it to him. This is important – he must not be allowed to snatch the food from its original position.

3 Repeat this until you are confident that your 'Leave it' command is working perfectly with the food in this new location and you no longer need to have your hand hovering by it.

Put on the polish
See if you can get your dog's eye contact during the 'Leave it' exercise. Where a dog looks is what he's thinking about.

Teach your dog in many different locations for him to understand the concept.

ADVANCED STAGES

When your dog has mastered the training exercises featured on pages 86–87, you can embark on these more advanced practices.

Food on the floor

This is the real test for many dogs. Food on the floor is always hard to resist, especially as we often encourage dogs to eat bits that we have dropped. Because of this, it is only reasonable to expect your dog to leave food on the floor if you have given him the command to do so.

1 Say 'Leave it' and then place a piece of food on the floor. Cup your hand around it, so you are ready to protect it if your dog comes forward to eat it. Click and give him a treat from your hand for leaving it.

2 Repeat this exercise, but gradually move your hand away from being near to the food.

3 When you are confident that your dog won't touch the food when you ask, repeat it, but this time lean your body away from it, so you aren't so close to it. However, be ready to guard it if necessary.

Note: Over several repetitions you should be able to tell your dog to leave the food on the floor and then move away from it. Always click and treat from your hand – he must never grab the food from the floor or he will be rewarded for performing the wrong behaviour.

Most dogs think food on the floor is theirs, so give your 'Leave it' cue early.

Take it further

You are now ready to tackle the most advanced version of this exercise: leaving thrown food.

1 Start the training session by standing in front of your dog and then tell him to 'Leave it'.

2 Throw a piece of food slightly behind you, so you block access to it with your body. Be ready to move to guard the food if you need to, either by covering it with your hand or your foot.

3 Click if your dog makes no attempt to get the food, and give him a treat from your hand before picking up the thrown treat.

Teaching your dog to leave a thrown treat improves his stay, and overall self-control.

Putting it into practice
There are 101 things and more that you probably don't want your dog to touch or pick up when he's out and about, such as cigarette ends and litter. In the home, too, there are items we don't want our dogs to touch – our shoes, the children's toys, or food on our plates. By practising the 'Leave it' command every day for a week, you will see great results. Practise for 14 days and you'll be amazed at what your dog can do.

CHAPTER 5
TEAM-BUILDING EXERCISES

Good trainers recognise they are living and working in partnership with their dog. Their relationship is enhanced because they realise that their dog is superior to them in some skills, by virtue of natural drive and instinct. The ultimate in teamwork is to let your dog take the lead whilst still retaining control, and there are many ways to practise this. Retrieving, scent work and target training are perhaps the best starter exercises; they also provide the foundations for many other aspects of training.

CATCH: FOOD AND TOYS

It seems that some dogs are naturals and are born to catch whereas others struggle to master this basic exercise. Catching is at the heart of many other behaviours, so although it may appear to be just a cute trick, its value in training is actually more progressive than this.

Catching food

There are a few simple guidelines that you should always follow when you start teaching your dog to catch a variety of food items and treats.

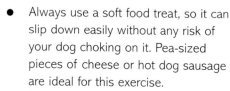

- Always use a soft food treat, so it can slip down easily without any risk of your dog choking on it. Pea-sized pieces of cheese or hot dog sausage are ideal for this exercise.
- Hold the treat between your thumb and forefinger right above your dog's nose – only 1–2cm (½–1in) away.
- Drop (don't throw) the food treat, so that all your dog has to do is open his mouth to catch it. It takes most dogs only three or four trials to work this out. If the treat bounces off his nose onto the floor, try to retrieve it before your dog does, as this can teach him to be lazy.

Some dogs are born catchers while others have to learn. Start with small, soft food treats and hold them right above your dog's nose. If your dog tries to grab the treat from your hand, go back to practising the leave cue.

- Once your dog is happily catching the food treat when you drop it from above his nose, you can start increasing the distance little by little until the treat is dropping vertically from 30cm (12in) or so.
- At this stage, you can add a gentle throwing action when you toss the treat. Build this up in such a way that your dog is having to make real efforts to catch the treat when you throw it.

Catching a toy

To teach your dog to catch a toy, just follow the same guidelines as outlined above, but this time use an object rather than a food treat.

- Start off with a soft, disposable cleaning cloth. Use just one sheet and tie it in a knot. This is lightweight and it won't hurt your dog if he fails to catch it.
- Drop it from only a tiny distance to begin with, and then build up gradually to real throws.
- As your dog gets better at catching, you can start using a favourite toy.

Once your dog is an expert at catching food, teach him to catch other articles – a soft knotted cloth is ideal to start with.

FETCH: TWO TOYS

If your dog loves chasing after toys but doesn't bring them back, this is for you. An informal fetch does not have to be perfect but he must bring the toy back and give it to you or place it within your reach. You should not have to tussle with him or chase after him.

Two-toy retrieve

This exercise works on the principles of reverse psychology – your dog will always want what you have. Follow the basic steps below.

1 Start off with two identical toys. This is essential because if the toys are different your dog may favour one over the other.

2 Play with one toy (hiding the other behind your back) and make sure your dog is eager to grab and tug it (see page 116). As soon as he's keen, throw it a short distance and encourage him to go and get it.

With one toy hidden behind your back, play with your dog with the other toy.

Throw the toy out for your dog to fetch – keep the other toy hidden behind your back for now.

3 When he has chased the toy and grabbed it, start playing excitedly with the toy you've kept: throw it into the air, stroke it or whirl it round you, while completely ignoring your dog.

4 Sooner or later, he will run over to try to get your toy, as it now looks more exciting than his. At this stage, he will have to drop his toy to play with yours.

5 Throw the toy you have been playing with and pick up the one your dog was carrying, and repeat the process. By doing this, you will always be in possession of one toy.

Play with the toy you're holding when your dog returns; he'll soon want to swap.

Team-building Exercises   95

FORMAL RETRIEVE

A formal retrieve is required for anyone who is planning to enter obedience competitions with their dog. However, its basic principle is also the cornerstone of many other training exercises and tricks, such as loading and unloading the washing machine or fetching a mobile phone or the television remote control.

Caution!
Never ever try to force your dog to keep any item in his mouth. Holding his muzzle closed around something will only make him want to spit it out more, not less.

Teaching the retrieve

Start off with an item that you know your dog will want to pick up and hold in his mouth. Most dogs enjoy picking up soft toys but you can also start off with a simple knotted piece of cloth.

1 You must start with your dog sitting in the heel position beside you (see page 46). He must stay in this position while you throw the article.

2 Using one command, you send your dog to fetch, and he will return to you, carrying the article to a position that is known as 'front present'.

3 Take the article (when told in competitions) and your dog returns to sit at heel.

Front present
Teaching the front present position is easiest done sitting down. Call your dog to you and encourage him to sit right between your feet, so that he is exactly facing you. Always click and treat for perfect positioning.

For a formal retrieve, your dog must sit at heel while you throw the article out.

Only once you have given the cue can your dog run out to fetch the article.

He should come to 'front present' while holding the article – without mouthing.

Once you have taken the article, your dog is sent to heel position once again.

SCENT WORK

In the wild, dogs hunt for food and search for water to drink. Their day is filled with scenting and searching activity, and sleep. In our domestic world, most dogs are effectively unemployed. We give them their food in a dish, water on tap, and walks only when and where we decide. Although our urban lifestyles place restraints on their outlets for natural behaviour, this does not mean that their ability to use their incredible sense of smell has been diminished.

Teaching your dog to use his nose in partnership with you can be wonderfully rewarding – this kind of scent work is a true test of teamwork.

All dogs, especially terriers and scent hounds, love to sniff when they are out walking. You can harness your dog's sense of smell in many games.

Your dog's world of scent

Dogs live in a world of scent, just like we live in a world of colour. For a dog, every trip to the park brings information via scent signals that other dogs have left. Although we might get frustrated that our dogs want to stop and sniff every few yards, it's the canine equivalent of reading the daily paper – and an integral part of being a dog.

Harnessing and utilising your dog's wonderful sense of smell is not very difficult but, like all dog training, it will get even better the more you practise. This is because, although your dog is already an expert, it will take some time for you to recognise his individual 'indicators' that tell you when he has found the search item.

Many dogs prefer food to toys, so encourage yours to find an article by putting treats inside a soft zip-up bag or pencil case.

Using a scent toy
If your dog is keen on toys, then choose one that you use only for scent work, and do not let him have access to it at any other time. If he is more food oriented, you can use a fluffy or soft zip-up pencil case or purse containing some smelly food, such as cheese.

HIDE AND SEEK: INDOOR SEARCHES

Like all training, the more you can transform any exercises into a game, the more your dog will enjoy doing them with you. Starting out on scent work is no different – and playing a traditional game of hide and seek is a great way to get him going.

Cup and treat

1 Ask your dog to sit for you while you place a tasty food treat under an old upturned cup or mug (don't use your best china).

2 Tell him to find the treat and then wait patiently and let him work out for himself how to get it.

Note: All dogs have different ways of approaching this dilemma. For instance, some will use their paws to push the cup over whereas others will use their nose or teeth to move it. Some genius dogs have even been known to pick up the cup by the handle. It's important that you take your time and allow your dog to work out how to solve this puzzle. If he gives up, simply lift the cup a tiny bit, so that he can see the treat again to renew his interest.

A working partnership

Sometimes you must learn to let your dog take the lead in training, although you still maintain control. In scent work, for instance, owners must rely almost entirely on their dog's incredible acuity to be able to detect and track a scent. Our sense of smell is very poor – we have approximately five million scent receptors in our noses whereas the average dog has over 200 million. It is said that a dog's ability to find even tiny molecules of scent is the equivalent of being able to detect a single grain of sand on a 10-metre square area of beach.

Hide the toy

1 Ask your dog to sit and stay in one room, or get a family member or friend to hold him, while you hide his 'scent toy' in another room. You can make the game relatively easy to begin with by hiding it in an obvious place, such as behind the sofa.

> ## Scent pools
> Scent has a life all of its own. It can create what is known as a scent 'pool', which, depending on wind, the temperature and other environmental factors, can be several metres, or even kilometres, away from the source.

2 Give your dog a release word and tell him to find. Praise him enthusiastically and have a good game with him or give him some treats when he finds the toy.

Training tip
As your dog becomes more proficient at this game, you can make it more challenging by increasing the difficulty of the hiding places as well as the duration that he has to sit and stay. This uses his brain and scenting abilities as well as helping him to practise impulse control – all in one.

It may seem simple but just learning to hunt for a special toy by scent alone can be complex for dogs that are used to searching by sight. It gives their brain a perfect work-out.

OUTDOOR MISSIONS

Once your dog has a good grasp of how to hunt for food and toys inside the house, the time has come to test his powers of scent outside. You can start off with these simple but enjoyable exercises.

Vehicle searches

Set up a mock 'drug search' on your car by having someone else conceal tiny pieces of your dog's favourite 'search food' around the exterior of the vehicle. Small pieces of cheese are perfect for this because they can be stuck to the rim of the wheel cover, the wheel arch or under the door handles.

- Keep your dog on a lead, and mind his claws on the paintwork.
- Always start and end at a fixed point – for example, the front left wheel.
- Assist your canine partner by walking backwards, with your dog in front of you. Use your hand to indicate where he should look next.

Vehicle searches can be great fun for both you and your dog.

Basic tracking

See if your dog can follow a scent trail to a search article or piece of food. Start on some fresh, untrodden grass, preferably first thing in the morning, as he will be able to follow the scent of crushed vegetation.

1 Lay a basic track. This means walking in a straight line for five to ten paces away from a pole to mark the start point. Once you have reached the end, turn on the spot and retrace one or two steps, then place your dog's 'scent toy' or a lidded container with some food in it on the track. Continue to retrace your steps back to the start point.

2 Put your dog's harness on him and then take him to the starting pole. Clip the line to the harness. If you consistently do this at the start point, he will learn that this is the signal for him to start tracking.

3 Indicate with your hand where the track starts. Let your dog sniff along the track until he finds the food or toy, then praise his clever behaviour lavishly.

Dogs are born to track. With very little training, he'll be able to follow simple scent trails.

TARGET TRAINING

Target training may not be on everyone's traditional list of dog training exercises, but it does provide us with the basis for many potential tasks and tricks – and it is also great for 'retraining' some of the basic commands, such as coming when called. The essence is teaching your dog to touch his nose or paw to an object or place on cue. Wherever you place this target thereafter, he will follow.

Teach your dog to touch your hand

The first stage of successful target training is to teach your dog to touch your hand. You can then progress to other objects (see page 106).

1 Hold out your hand so that the palm is flat and the fingers are held together. Keep it in a vertical position and present it to your dog, slightly to the side of his face.

2 Watch him carefully; the chances are that he will immediately turn his head to look at your hand or sniff it. Click and give him a treat as soon as he does so, and remove your hand.

3 Repeat this several times, watching for your dog to touch his nose to your hand and clicking and giving a treat each time he does.

Hand touching is the perfect way to embark on target training of all types, and can also be used to improve your dog's recall.

4 Most dogs will need at least 10 to 20 repetitions of this behaviour before they fully understand the concept of 'touch nose to hand'.

5 Now you can start to move your hand. Position it slightly higher, so your dog has to reach up to touch it. Move it lower, so he has to bend down. Click and treat for good responses.

Recall training

Hand targeting can also work beautifully for recall training. Instead of calling your dog by name, just ask him to touch your hand – he'll have to come to you to perform the task and get his click and treat.

On cue

To get the behaviour 'on cue', say the word 'Touch' just before you present your hand. Repeat this until you are confident that your dog will touch your hand no matter what position you put it in.

Taking it further

Many complex tasks can be taught as a result of the easy-to-learn basics. Indeed, service dogs or assistance dogs are trained using these methods, so they can develop the skills and independence of mind required to help their disabled owners. Therefore if you would like to train your dog to close the door behind him when he comes into a room, switch lights on and off, tidy up his toys, or even load and unload the washing machine, these exercises are the perfect way to start.

BULL'S EYE

Train your dog to hit the bull's eye by teaching him to touch his paw or nose to a target object. This can be as simple as the lid from a tub of margarine initially. It is sensible to use a disposable object as some dogs may try to grab or bite at the target at the outset. Remember that good target training is all about timing, so make sure that you have everything you need to hand before you begin the training session.

Touch the target

1 Present the target vertically slightly to the side of your dog's face. Be ready to click the instant he sniffs at it. Take the target away immediately.

2 Present the target again, and click for a touch. Remember that the click tells your dog what it was that got him the reward, so you don't have to be in a hurry to give him the food treat.

3 Repeat this process, gradually moving the target so that it is more challenging for your dog to touch it.

4 When you are confident that he will touch the target as soon as it is presented, add your cue word – 'Touch' – just before presenting it.

'Twofers'

At this stage of training, make your dog work harder for his reward. Ask him to touch the target but do not click and treat. Instead, prompt him to repeat the behaviour, only clicking and treating once he has performed two good responses. This is called a 'twofer' as he will have performed 'two for one' click and treat. If you feel ambitious, try a 'threefer', too.

Remote targets
When your dog is an expert at touching the target held in your hand, move on to training with 'remote' targets by taping the target object to a wall, the back of a door or on the floor.

Train your dog to touch a target – either with his nose as shown here, or with a paw. This can lead to all kinds of target training possibilities.

Practical uses of target training

The world is your oyster once your dog can touch a target with his nose or paw. Have a think about which tricks or training exercises you can use it for. A nose touch to a button can be a way to teach him to press a switch, while a push with a front paw easily translates into teaching him to close an open door. One of my favourite exercises involves training a dog to touch one back paw to a small piece of white tape. From this, you can teach your dog to pretend to cock his leg on cue – perfect for film work or a great party trick.

SEND OUT

Teaching your dog to do a 'send out' is a practical application of target training. It can make up part of your training for the 'send-away' – an obedience exercise in which the dog is instructed to run away from his handler in a straight line until he is told to stop and lie down. It can also be useful for free tracking, when you direct your dog towards a hedge or tree to start searching for a 'lost' item, or just a good way of giving him some more exercise – as he has to run out to touch a target in the distance and then run back to you.

What to do

Start your 'send out' training indoors where there are few distractions, but move it as quickly as possible to an outdoor location for maximum results.

1 Choose your 'send-out' target. This should be easily visible for your dog even when it is some distance away in long grass. A cone or bollard is perfect for this exercise.

2 Start your target training in exactly the same way as you did with your hand (see page 104) or the lid (see page 106). Put the cone in front of your dog. Remember that the first time he sees it he will naturally want to sniff it, so be ready with your clicker or to say your clicker word.

3 As soon as your dog is touching the new target, ask him for two behaviours before clicking and treating – 'Touch' and 'Down'.

4 When he will offer you a touch and then an instant down on command, gradually move the cone further away, little by little. Build up slowly and reward those successes generously.

> ### Click and treat
> The click, or clicker word, tells your dog that he's done the right thing, so even when he's at a distance from you, you can click and then walk up to your dog to give him the treat.

Setting your dog up for a send-out. Your dog needs to be facing the correct way and must wait for your command before running out to the marker.

Once your dog reaches the marker, another cue may be given – in this case 'Down'. The dog must then wait patiently until you call him back again.

CHAPTER 6

USING YOUR DOG'S INSTINCTS

A close relationship between man and dog has endured through thousands of years. Our pet dogs live with us as our closest friends and confidantes, but we must never forget that they are a separate species, with skills, needs and desires all of their own. Dogs are born with the inherent blueprint to be dogs and they have no qualms about expressing normal canine behaviours, such as barking, digging, slobbering and leaping around. By allowing your dog to develop his natural drives and abilities in an appropriate way, he will have a 'natural' opportunity to express his instincts and you can reap the rewards in terms of his responsiveness and enjoyment.

DIGGING INDOORS

Many dogs, particularly young ones and terriers, just love to dig. The dilemma is that while this may be a natural instinct for your dog, it is not always compatible with having a beautiful garden, unless you appreciate it looking like a golf course. While it may be tempting simply to try and deter your dog from digging, his 'hard wired' behaviour needs an appropriate outlet, so providing one can save both of you a lot of stress. Here are some practical strategies for you to try out to prevent unwanted behaviours.

It's in the box

To encourage your dog to enjoy an acceptable indoor digging habit, place a food treat in the bottom of a shallow cardboard box. Let him see you do this, then cover the treat with some scrunched-up paper or a sheet of cardboard. Allow him to investigate the box thoroughly, climb inside it and dig for the treat.

Digging for gold
Some owners worry that giving their dog a place to dig will actually encourage the habit. However, the rewards that your dog gets for digging in his one special area will ensure that he's less likely to dig anywhere else.

Many terriers and other breeds, such as Dachshunds, have been bred to dig. Offering indoor opportunities for this behaviour will resolve frustration and give your dog an appropriate outlet for this natural behaviour.

Make it more fun

Once your dog can perform this exercise successfully, you can make it increasingly more challenging by doing one of the following things.

- Use a smaller cardboard box inside a larger one, with treats sandwiched between the two.
- Make the cardboard box larger and taller.
- Use a toy inside the box rather than a treat – hide it under some sheets of scrunched-up newspaper or old towels.

Puzzle toys of all kinds help to keep your dog occupied and out of mischief. This Golden Retriever enjoys chewing on a Kong toy, which has been filled with some of his usual food.

Safety first

Always ensure that the box you use is clean and free from any tape or staples that could hurt your dog's mouth or paws.

Match the size of the box to your dog's height and capabilities. Make it simple and inviting initially – it can become more complex as time goes on.

DIGGING OUTDOORS

Digging is work for idle paws and, all in all, most dogs only dig outdoors because they are bored. It's a satisfying occupation for a dog without any other job to do, and the attention they get from their owners – even if it's negative – is just the icing on the cake.

Digging rules

If you want to prevent your dog from digging in your yard or garden, there are a few basic rules that you must understand:

- Some specific breeds or types of dog need to dig as part of their natural behavioural repertoire. Terriers, in particular, need outlets for this natural behaviour – it's what they were bred to do.
- If you intend to leave your dog outside without supervision, you must give him things to do to keep him occupied, or he will bark, chew your plants and dig. A Kong toy, filled with food treats, can be perfect as it takes time and effort for your dog to empty it.
- Telling dogs off for digging will not stop the behaviour – in fact, it often makes it worse by virtue of the fact that they get attention from their owners for doing the 'wrong' thing.

If your dog is landscaping your lawn, focus his digging in a single area.

Creating a digging pit outdoors

You can channel your dog's natural digging instincts into a more acceptable, appropriate behaviour by giving him his own place to dig.

- Choose an area for your dog to dig in. This could be part of a flower bed or a child's large sandpit. Fill it with loose sand.
- Take your dog to this area every day and let him watch while you hide goodies, such as bones, chews or toys, in there.
- Allow him to dig in this area.

Digging is a natural instinct for all dogs – and a strong breed drive for terriers.

TUGGING

Contrary to popular belief, teaching your dog to play with you with a toy will not make him aggressive or challenging. Instead, you will be giving him an appropriately controlled outlet for this natural behaviour. It will also act as another useful 'tool' in your essential 'toolkit' of rewards, which you can use in training. As most dogs have sharp teeth, fast reactions and a drive to chase and catch their 'prey', it is extremely important that tug games are only ever played by the rules.

Rule 1

Always keep the toy on the floor. It can whizz about, like a prey animal trying to get away from the dog, or it can act like a snake to engage his interest, but it must stay low to the ground. Bringing the toy up near your face will mean that your dog's

Many dogs love to tug – some have a compulsion to do so. Teaching them to abide by the rules makes this safe.

> ### Motivating your dog
> If your dog is reluctant to play, move the toy away from him slowly, as if it were a snake. Make it disappear behind the furniture and then reappear again briefly. This will make it almost irresistible to him.

mouth and teeth will move towards your face, too, so keep the toy low, no matter how exciting the game becomes for your dog.

Rule 2

Your dog must never put his teeth on you, even by accident. If he does, you must finish the game instantly. In addition, make sure that you march out of the room in an award-winning performance of disgust at your dog's rudeness. This will help to reinforce the message.

Suitable tug toys

Tug games always need to be played with a long rope or a fleece tug toy. This keeps your fingers safe and well away from your dog's mouth. Never allow anyone in the family to play tug using their clothing or as part of a wrestling game.

Play sounds

Many dogs like to growl during tug play. This is not a problem as long as you can trust your dog to let go of the toy by using one quiet command – and he always obeys you.

Rule 3

Your dog must let go of the toy instantly on one quiet command. This keeps the game safe, because no matter how excited he gets when playing, you will be able to control him. Make sure you choose a command word and stick to it.

Tugging does not have to be competitive – it should be fun for both of you.

TEACHING DOGS TO LET GO

You need to ensure that your dog will relinquish the toy as soon as you tell him to do so. This will keep you in control and make the game safe, no matter who is playing with him. The command you give your dog to release the toy can be any word you choose, such as 'Give' or 'Drop'.

Essential guidelines

1 Always play enthusiastically with your dog with his tug toy, so that he is really committed to the game.

2 After a moment or so, quietly say the word 'Give' and then drop a tasty food treat right in his line of vision, under his muzzle.

3 As soon as he releases the toy to eat the food, praise him and tell him how good he is. At this point, you should not even attempt to touch the toy but leave it where he has dropped it. Once he has finished eating the treat, you can start playing tug again.

4 Repeat this exercise at least five times in quick succession, using short bursts of play and then encouraging your dog to drop the toy in return for a tasty food titbit.

5 On the sixth game, say the word 'Give' without putting a food treat down, and see if your dog drops the toy. If he does so, praise him immediately and have another good game. If he seems unsure about letting go of the toy, resume using the treat as a lure for another four or five tries.

Toys versus food

Some dogs love playing and prefer a game to a food treat. If yours is one of these and he won't relinquish the toy for even the tastiest treat, such as a piece of cheese or some hot dog sausage, then you will need to use another identical toy as the lure to train him to drop the first one (see pages 96–97).

Teaching your dog to drop the tug toy when you ask is essential. Engage him in a good game to begin with.

When you are ready, drop some really tasty food treats on the floor under your dog's nose. Do not remove the toy when he drops it to eat the treats.

After eating the treats, he should wait politely to resume the game. Stop at once if he tries to grab you or the toy.

AGILITY AND GARDEN GAMES

Whether you have ambitions to compete with your dog in agility competitions or you just want to increase your outdoor control with him, garden games and agility can be extremely helpful and a great introduction. Here are some suggestions to get you started.

Basic hurdles

You can buy basic plastic hurdles from children's toy shops or on the internet, but really you need nothing more sophisticated than two upturned flower pots and a bamboo cane. The hurdle needs to be low to begin with, as even big dogs need to learn where their back feet are.

1 Ask your dog to sit to one side of the hurdle while you go to the other side and face him.

2 Call him over the jump and click as his front feet take off. You can give him a tasty treat or a game with a toy to reward him for good attempts.

Tunnel vision

Most dogs just love running through a tunnel once they have built up their confidence, but never assume that your dog will accomplish this task without practising first. Children's play tunnels are cheap and widely available. However, they do have to be pegged down for safety – this will not only keep them stable but also will prevent them rolling or moving.

1 Start by squashing up the tunnel so that your dog only has to step through an enlarged 'hoop'. Click and treat.

When they are taught carefully, most dogs love running through the agility tunnel.

2 When he can do this, make the tunnel a little longer, and click and treat again, gradually building on your success.

3 When your dog is going into the tunnel with gusto, fully extend it, so that he has to run right through to get his reward.

Weave heaven

Setting up weave poles in your home or garden couldn't be easier – you can use homemade or pre-bought ones. To start, stagger the poles in a zig-zag fashion, setting them between 50 and 60cm (20 and 24in) apart, with the poles angled outwards at about 45 degrees. Your dog should be able to run down the central 'path' between the poles. Practise this until he's really confident before bringing the poles into one central straight line, and before raising each pole to an upright position.

It's worth spending time teaching your dog to run down the central 'path' between weave poles that are angled outwards and staggered in spacing. This helps him to understand that accuracy is more important than speed.

Using Your Dog's Instincts   121

PARK FUN AND URBAN AGILITY

Combine training and off-lead fun with your dog in the local park with some canine 'parkour'. You can even practise agility in an urban environment. Here are some ideas to get you inspired.

Le parkour

A park bench can make a good starter 'obstacle' – you can teach your dog to:
- Hop up and sit on the bench.
- Hop up and lie down on the bench.
- Run around the bench in a clockwise direction.
- Run around the opposite way.
- Limbo dance under the bench on command.
- Lie quietly next to the bench and settle down, while you sit on it and have a drink, snack or rest.

Urban agility

The concrete jungle can be transformed into a creative agility course for your city-dwelling hound – although it does take a little imagination.
- Bollards or traffic cones: teach your dog to weave in and out of them. This is the city equivalent of weaving poles in the agility field.
- Kerbs and low walls: teach your dog to walk on the kerb or on top of a low wall. Click and treat for all four paws on. This is good practice from a safety point of view and also teaches him balance and agility. Use lots of praise and the motivation of a food treat if you need it.

> ### Note
> Always avoid children's play areas or any place where dogs are prohibited, and remember to show due consideration to other people in the area – not everyone loves dogs.

This Cocker Spaniel has been trained to get on and off a park bench on cue.

USEFUL INFORMATION

Wonderful websites

Association of Pet Dog Trainers (UK)
www.apdt.co.uk
The Association of Pet Dog Trainers is an organisation that promotes the highest standards of positive dog training in the UK. All members are assessed according to a strict Code of Practice. Find a local trainer via their regional map, or be inspired to join in with a dog sport, such as Rally (see opposite).

Association of Pet Behaviour Counsellors
www.apbc.org.uk
Full members are specialists who work on veterinary referral, helping with behavioural problems in pets. Visit the website for details of your nearest member.

Clever Dog Company
www.cleverdogcompany.com
Sarah Whitehead's website – featuring lots of free downloads on behaviour and training, as well as video clips and practical suggestions for a harmonious relationship with your dog.

Clickertraining.com
www.clickertraining.com
Karen Pryor's excellent website focusing on all things clicker training.

Dog Star Daily
www.dogstardaily.com
Fab dog blog featuring behaviour and training experts from around the globe.

Talk Dog
www.thinkdog.org
Find out what your dog is really saying! A three-month home-study course using DVD material focusing on canine body language and facial expression.

Train your dog online
www.trainyourdogonline.com
Train your dog with video lessons in the comfort of your own home.

Dog sports to inspire
Agility
www.the-kennel-club.org.uk
Dogs negotiate an obstacle course off-lead in a race for both time and accuracy. The handler is not allowed to touch or lure the dog in any way. Obstacles include the 'A frame', the see-saw, dogwalk and tunnel.

Flyball
www.flyball.org.uk
Flyball is run, in teams of four dogs, as a relay. Dogs race against each other from a start line away from their handlers over a series of hurdles to a box that releases a tennis ball. The dogs must then catch the ball and run back to their handlers while carrying the ball.

Heelwork to music
www.maryray.co.uk
The handler and dog perform heelwork in a choreographed routine, demonstrating flair and style to suit both dog and handler. 'Freestyle' routines allow other moves and more interpretation of the music.

Obedience
www.the-kennel-club.org.uk
There are six levels of competitive obedience, from Pre-Beginners right up to Class C. The exercises in each range from heelwork (on and off the lead) to recall and control exercises, such as a one-minute sit and a two-minute down-stay. The advanced class includes exercises, such as scent discrimination and send-away.

Rally
www.apdt.co.uk
Each dog and handler navigate a course with numbered signs indicating different exercises to perform, such as: Sit-Down-Sit, Straight Figure 8, Send over Jump, Recall over Jump and Left Turn. All dogs – purebred, mixed breed and dogs with disabilities – are encouraged to participate.

Scentwork
**www.thinkdog.org /
www.talkingdogs.org.uk**
Dogs are trained to search for specific scents – these are then hidden in structured patterns of obstacles in varying environments. While scentwork is a recognised sport in the USA, it is only now becoming more popular in the UK for pet dogs.

Further reading

Donaldson, Jean, *The Culture Clash*
(1996) ISBN: 18880470504 (James & Kenneth Publishers)

Eaton, Barry, *Dominance - fact or fiction?*
(2008) ISBN: 9780953303946

Fisher, John, *Diary of A Dotty Dog Doctor*
(1998) ISBN: 095328140X (Alpha Publishing)

McConnell, Patricia, *For the Love of a Dog: Understanding Emotion in You and Your Best Friend*
(2007) ISBN: 9780345477156 (Ballantine Books)

Pryor, Karen, *Don't Shoot the Dog*
(2002) ISBN: 1860542387 (Ringpress Books)

Pryor, Karen, *Reaching the Animal Mind*
(2009) ISBN: 9780743297769 (Scribner)

Ray, Mary, and Harding, Justine, *Dog Tricks: Fun and Games for Your Clever Canine*
ISBN: 978-0600611776 (Hamlyn)

Top of the class watching

Dog training lesson in a box – Your Clever Dog DVD series – unique problem solving on DVD for specific issues: pulling on lead, coming when called, house training, jumping up and over-excitability, puppy biting and basic clicker training. www.yourcleverdog.com

The Motivation Movie DVD – 37 min DVD, by Joanna Hill, inspirational UK obedience trainer. ISBN: 053281493. www.dogtrain.co.uk

INDEX